TURNER'S TAOISIGH

My Brush With Kildare Street

IRISH TIMES BOOKS

Published by: The Irish Times Limited (Irish Times Books)
Design & Layout: Angelo McGrath

© The Irish Times Limited 2014
Text © Martyn Turner 2014
Cartoons © Martyn Turner, except cartoon on page 22 © Andy Davey
ISBN 978-0-9070-1139 2

INTRODUCTION

So then I thought: "It's time I did another book". I miss the smell of a newly printed, freshly minted tome. And then I thought that Mr Editor seemed to like the little bits and stories wot i rote when we, er, celebrated my 40 years after the masthead 3 years ago. So then I thought about the publisher who we once gave a lift to the airport who said, languishing in the opulent back seat of our German motor: "Why don't you write a memoir. I'd publish it". He was, of course, under the misguided opinion that I had done other things in my life than sit in a darkened room everyday and crank out another drawing. And play golf twice a week. Of course I haven't. And anyway I was well aware that Her Indoors, sitting next to me in the car when he said that 'write a memoir' thing was thinking, in 10 foot high letters, "OVER MY DEAD BODY". So this isn't a memoir. Certainly not, heaven forbid. It isn't a history. But it has memories and potted historical facts. It is just a few bits and pieces written down about the nine Taoisigh I have had the.......what would be the word? Honour? No. Distinction? No. Pleasure, no, not really.......had the necessity to work under since I moved to Dublin in 1976 to contribute an almost daily cartoon to The Irish Times. Not being a journalist, I am exempt from actually having to check anything that I write so, in advance, I apologise if I have got anything wrong. And also, in these straightened times, I have added value, as one is supposed to do, says Mrs Merkel. Apart from reprinting a bunch of old cartoons that go with the various governments, I have attempted - through a long gruelling May - to paint new portraits of the gents in question. Without the safety net of looking at their pictures. just out of my head. With real watercolours and brushes and pencils. The lot. No expense spared. No, please, don't thank me. Buying the book is enough reward. If I had waited a couple of years, days, hours (who knows with Irish politics) I could have called it Turner's Ten Taoisigh. But there's only nine of the ba...blessed people; Cosgrave, Lynch, Haughey, FitzGerald, Bruton, Reynolds. Ahern, Cowen and Enda.

If I had been a bit more proactive, withering and aggressive down the years, I could have called it - stealing from Spike Milligan – "Taoisigh -My Part in Their Downfall". But I'm not arrogant enough to suggest it. Just arrogant enough to mention it.
Martyn Turner

Ps. I have tried, wherever possible, to print cartoons here that haven't appeared in any of my other books. The length of the chapters reflect, generally, the length of time each Taoiseach was in office. Thus Bertie gets far more coverage than anyone else. Liam Cosgrave's taoiseachship had only been going a wet weekend (as far as I was concerned) when he was replaced by Jack Lynch. Thus there are few cartoons of Cosgrave in my files, folders, old books and corners of the studio. So I have included a few cartoons about his cabinet from that time. They were probably the most interesting thing about his term of office.

Liam Cosgrave

March 1973 until July 1977. Liam Cosgrave became Taoiseach, reluctantly if the title of one of his biographies is correct, after a general election in March 1973. He had been a TD since 1943. He led a coalition government between Fine Gael and the Labour Party. Fine Gael cabinet members included Garret FitzGerald, Peter Barry, Richie Ryan, Paddy Cooney, Paddy Donegan and, briefly, Oliver J. Flanagan. Labour ministers included Conor Cruise O'Brien, Michael O'Leary, Justin Keating and their leader Brendan Corish

S ometime early in 1976 - February would be my guess - I was invited down to Dublin to lunch with the then editor of The Irish Times, Fergus Pyle. He offered me a job, sort of. They wanted me to draw more cartoons every week (I was already contributing a couple a week) and they would pay me a retainer, not much, and they would pay me for a whole year whether I lasted the course or not. How could I refuse? It was what I wanted to do.

For various reasons, one of which involved a field of potatoes I was nurturing, I didn't start this one year experiment until the following September. By then I had realised that even though, after almost 10 years of living in Belfast, studying at Queens and working as one of the editors of 'Fortnight' magazine, I knew almost everything there was to know about 40 shades of orange and 60 shades of 'Republicanism' but I had not a clue about the 40 shades of green that was politics in the Republic of Ireland. I did not know, for example, the difference between Fine Gael and Fianna Fáil. Forty years on, of course, I still don't know the difference but now it is not out of ignorance but out of exasperation at civil war politics.

Liam Cosgrave was Taoiseach; a quiet grey man with little charisma which was probably an ideal character trait for someone who had to hold together the disparate bunch of larger than life politicians from both Labour and Fine Gael that made up his government. There were rogue elements within his own party who were, heaven forfend, somewhat liberal and embraced Declan Costello's treatise 'The Just Society' which essentially argued that social change was a necessity and not just a luxury that could be looked at when economic indicators were favourable.

I remember all this guff because the first cartoon I drew under this new relationship with the paper was about Cosgrave and the "mongrel foxes" as the social wing of Fine Gael was known. It was not, and is not, my best idea. In fact it was pretty appalling but, hey, I was a neophyte, nervous and - not to put too fine a point on it - panic stricken.

The Irish Times ran the cartoon on the front page (or the main page as we newshounds call it) by way of

introduction to their new free transfer signing. I suspect day two's effort was buried at the bottom of page 26.

By Christmas that year any fears I might have had that a) Irish politics was too boring to sustain a daily cartoon and b) that I would struggle to think up a daily cartoon had been pretty much dispelled (in my own mind – I can't speak for the readers). That was further enhanced the following year when Liam Cosgrave marched into the opposition side of the house to vote against his own government's Contraception Bill. Wow, I thought, in Irish politics anything can happen and usually does.

I never met Liam Cosgrave but I once stood about two rows behind him in the stand at Punchestown. My father was over from England for the races and he was bemused as I had just been introduced, by Charlie McCreevy, to someone else as "a fine Kildare man".(Charlie was as wrong about that as he was to prove to be about economic theory) My father asked "Who was that?" and I said "The Minister for Finance". "Blimey, and he is just running around here without any security?" he said being used to the ways of Westminster ministers. "Yes," I said, "it is normal here", and paused to look around "and see that guy there? He's the Minister for Agriculture and that bloke two rows down, he used to be Prime Minister."

Party Animals.. in rough order top to bottom, left to right; Paddy Hillery, Johnny Giles, Garret FitzGerald, Henry Kissinger, Ian Smith, John Taylor, Cearbhall O'Dalaigh, Gerald Ford, John Kelly (who seems to be in the drawing three times), Willie John McBride, Jimmy Carter, Chairman Mao, Valerie Giscard D'Estaing, Michael O'Leary, Conor Cruise O'Brien, Brendan Corish, Merlyn Rees, Jack Lynch, Charles Haughey, Denis Healey (when I was a child I used to play golf with an old gentleman who claimed to be his father. This is one of the most obscure facts in this book. In this universe), Richie Ryan, Gordon, an electrician friend from Belfast, Dominc Turner aged 3, Paddy Donegan, Liam Cosgrave, Oliver Flanagan, Dick Burke, Someone or other..haven't the foggiest, Justin Keating, Enoch Powell and Paddy Cooney.

The drawing is slightly altered from the original as The Irish Times asked me to change a bottle in someone's hand to a cracker as they didn't wish to imply a politician might be a bit fond of the drink. I had a similar 'incident' when I drew a weekly cartoon for the Sunday News in Belfast. I drew Paddy Devlin of the SDLP, with a pint of Guinness in his hand. The paper, without telling me, sort of painted it out of the cartoon in such a way as it was quite obvious that someone had painted something out. They told me the same thing. Don't like to imply politicians drink.

Coincidentally Paddy Devlin spoke in Stormont a few weeks later on the subject of the Licensing Laws. He said, I paraphrase, that if the pubs were open 24 hours a day that wouldn't be long enough for him.

Cosgrave's Ministers

Conor Cruise O'Brien

Conor Cruise O'Brien was the Minister for Posts and Telegraphs in the coalition government. Astonishingly for a journalist and broadcaster and former advocate of free speech, he introduced what they call 'draconian' legislation to try to rid the airways of Provos and their fellow travellers. It was less draconian and more plain daft when it came to be implemented.

It is a difficult area. I remember when we lived in Northern Ireland that some journalists in the BBC and UTV were concerned that reporting such stuff as "there's a riot going on in the Lower Falls", for example, was only encouraging people from outside the Lower Falls to drop over and join in. I think they proposed a ban on reporting live events and waiting until the results were in.

The Cruiser's regulations just led to work for actors to do voice overs of, say, Gerry Adams who was never in the IRA - please don't ever forget that - but who was always good for a bit of Provo explanation and cheer leading.

I had dinner with Dr O'Brien once. He wouldn't remember. I was part of a group of Northern Ireland media who were invited to Dublin and the border to see how the Republic's government was dealing with subversives.

As the evening wore on and the excellent wine cellar of the Department of Foreign Affairs was marginally depleted, we fell into having a jolly good row with the minister. Quite exciting it was and quite informative too.

I was never invited back. Years later I met a retired civil servant who was Secretary of the Department at some stage. We talked about that night and I said: "it's odd but I was never invited back". "No," he said, "they have a file about you". It says "bit of a problem, or some such..". "But," he added, as he watched me fill my plate with salad, "I don't know whether it was because of your behaviour or the fact you are a vegetarian."

Oliver J Flanagan

Oliver J was a caricature of a blueshirt. Devoutly Catholic, he once claimed that sex had been invented by television in 1963. Whether he had the age or the inclination to be a member of Eoin O'Duffy's fascist irregulars, it has been reported that he made a speech in the Dáil in 1943 suggesting that all Jews should be thrown out of the country. So he was on the right, the extreme right, wavelength. He was a perpetual canvasser who usually topped the poll in his constituency. It was said he would visit the local council offices and check out where the council workmen would be labouring, fixing and mending in the forthcoming weeks. He then canvassed the area they were going to and when some constituent complained about the potholes in the roads or whatever, he would note it down and say he would get them fixed straight away. Sure enough the council labourers soon turned up. He was briefly made Minister for Defence by Liam Cosgrave. Clearly his love of Army guns surpassed his Christian principles, you know the ones that go on about 'thou shall not kill'.

Paddy Donegan

Donegan was the Minister for Defence who caused a constitutional crisis. Whilst making a speech somewhere down the country, he deviated from script to deliver a broadside in the direction of the President, Cearbhall Ó Dálaigh. He called him a "thundering disgrace" for referring some piece of anti-terrorist legislation to the Supreme Court - as was his right. In the ensuing kerfuffle, Liam Cosgrave refused to accept Mr Donegan's offer to resign. So the President resigned

Some lines on the occasion of a Ministerial speech at Mullingar

While addressing the troops bold and handsome,
His pre-arranged speech overran some,
The T.D. from Louth,
Put his foot in his mouth
And spoke out the back of his transom.

Richie Ryan

Richie Ryan was the Minister for Finance who had to oversee the post oil crisis economy. A bit like the situation Michael Noonan found himself in a few years ago. He was another quiet sort of unassuming person, like his Taoiseach. I received a hand written letter from him one day requesting the original of a cartoon I had drawn. I replied with terms and conditions and he replied with a hand written cheque. I sent the cartoon and he wrote yet again, with his own stamp in his own handwriting, thanking me. I stress those last two things as in all this time, with many requests from politicians for drawings or prints, he was the only person who wrote on his own paper, with his own stamp and in his own way. Everyone else has either made contact through a civil servant or on a government funded sheet of paper or in some other taxpayer subsidised way.

I thought well of him for this, and then I met him. At Strasbourg airport when I was coming back from a trip to the European parliament and he likewise. He was a MEP at that stage. I introduced myself and we chatted pleasantly for a while. He sort of reminded me of my father-in-law. Then I happened to mention one of the other MEPs, an Ulster Unionist, thinking he might sigh deeply and express some sort of wish for love and understanding amongst fellow Irishmen. Far from it. I got an earful of expletives about the man and his politics. I didn't think any less of him for it. I was just surprised and I'm not often surprised.

Jack Lynch

Jack Lynch was Taoiseach twice. Firstly from November 1966 until March 1973. He then "stole" the 1977 election from the Cosgrave coalition which was expected to be re-elected. He served as Taoiseach with the Fianna Fáil government from July 1977 until he resigned as party leader in December 1979. Amongst his more notable cabinet members in his second spell were George Colley (Minister for Finance) and Charles Haughey (Minister for Health).

ack Lynch hardly impinged on our life in Northern Ireland when he was Taoiseach for 7 years in the late sixties and early seventies. We had too much to worry about on our own doorstep as a valid and necessary Civil Rights movement transmogrified and deformed at the edges into an excuse for tribal mass murder.

And then in 1969, following some pogroms and the like, and a string of Catholic refugees heading to the Republic, he made a speech suggesting UN peace keeping intervention (probably a good idea) and immediate talks with the British government on the unification of the island (probably not a good idea. The British government was never the problem. Most British people would divest themselves of the responsibility of governing Northern Ireland in the morning and bung you a great lump of money for your trouble. It was, and is, the Unionists the Republic has to assuage).

The speech also included the phrase "the Irish Government can no longer stand by and see innocent people injured and perhaps worse". This was re-quoted on all sides in the North as "we will not stand idly by" and was interpreted widely and wildly that the Irish Army would be invading at any minute. This would not have been a good idea.

It also seemed to lead, logically, to the illegal plan to import weapons, which led to the Arms Crisis in 1970 and the subsequent Arms Trial. Charles Haughey and Neil Blaney were sacked from the Government. Jim Gibbons and Jack Lynch came out of the episode relatively unscathed.

What is clear is that someone, lots of people, were lying. Strangely two of the potential liars, Haughey and Gibbons, were in Lynch's second government in 1977. He couldn't tell who was telling porkies so he gave them both, like the jury at the Arms Trial, the benefit of the doubt. That's politics for you. There has been recent evidence that both Lynch and Gibbons knew more about the affair than they had ever let on. I asked a chum, who used to be a politician, poor luv, "who lied?" and he said "Everyone"….

My first contact with Jack Lynch, professionally wise, cartoon wise, Irish Times wise, was in 1973 when Ireland joined the European Community. I had been contributing cartoons and caricatures to The Irish Times since the summer of 1971 but my areas of work were confined to the Northern pages and the foreign pages. This was my first venture into 'domestic' politics and I was commissioned to do a vast drawing celebrating the arrival of the saints and scholars of Ireland into mainland Europe.

I rushed into Belfast the day Ireland became European to buy a copy of the paper and see where my drawing was. The answer was nowhere. In a large white space somewhere in the paper was a copy of the cover of the accession treaty. I had committed the offense, apparently, of placing a halo over the head of Jack Lynch (I had assumed he was a saint, not a scholar) and the drawing had been removed from the paper so someone could go to work excising the offending small white circle. Making a hole instead of a holy halo, I guess.

The drawing appeared in the next day's edition, cleansed.

It was apparent that Jack Lynch was held in incredibly high regard by all and sundry. I was more accustomed to politicians being held in low regard, and in Northern Ireland and Britain not without reason. He seemed to be quite charismatic, partly because of his prowess in an earlier life as a GAA star and partly because of the matter of fact way he went about things. He had a wonderful soft Cork way of speaking. I think the word 'avuncular' covers it which is defined as the sort of man you would like as an uncle or a grandfather.

When I was working in Dublin in the late '70s Jack Lynch caused a small crisis of my own. For the first and only time in my 4 decades of contributing political cartoons to the paper, I received what could be considered political direction from the editors of *The Irish Times*. I repeat, for those of you out there (on the internet mostly, where idiots with keyboards gather and dream up conspiracies) for the first and ONLY time did I receive what could be classed as political direction from The Irish Times when Douglas Gageby, the editor, said to me one day "Do you have to piss on Jack Lynch? Can you not just expend your bile on foreigners?"

I'm not sure how I reacted. Knowing me, I adopted my usual stance in such situations; kept my head down, remained silent and got on with it expecting, daily, to be relieved of my duties. It's pretty much how I operate today. The life of a political cartoonist (freelance) is not a secure one.

Being ignorant of the ways of the world I went to see someone in the Educational Building Society whose offices were adjacent to the Irish Times premises on D'Olier Street. It is where Irish Times people, I was told, went for mortgages.

"Can I have a mortgage, please, Mr EBS?"

"What do you do for a living?"

"I'm a freelance political cartoonist," I said, adding "with a one year contract with *The Irish Times.*"

He laughed and waved me away. No one laughs at my cartoons but they laugh at the idea of me drawing cartoons. I'll take whatever I can get.

Desperate for funds to buy a semi derelict farmhouse in Kildare I rang the bank in England where my wife, and now us both, had an account.

"Could you lend me some money to buy a house, please? We are moving to southern Ireland."

(No need for territorial nomenclatural niceties when talking to English people.)

"Sure," he said, "why are you moving?"

"*The Irish Times* in Dublin have offered me a contract."

"Oh, great," he said "we had been wondering when you would get a job."

15

⸺ Charles J. Haughey ⸺

Charlie Haughey was Taoiseach three times. Firstly after he took over the leadership of Fianna Fáil from Jack Lynch in December 1979 and led the government until June 1981. He had another brief bash at the job between March and December 1982. Thirdly, lastly, and longly (!) he ran the country (into the ground) from March 1987 until February 1992. He was first elected to the Dáil in 1957.

uch has been written about Charlie Haughey. And there will be much more. He even had a large lump of a tribunal devoted to his ability to gather donations to maintain his personal lifestyle whilst in office. "Thanks for the cheque, big fella."

His wealth, maybe his debts, were accumulated in full public view. One only had to look at the lack of trappings of wealth in the lifestyle of his immediate contemporary Brian Lenihan to wonder where the money came from. Their backgrounds and parliamentary careers were almost parallel yet Lenihan lived in a semi in Castleknock and Haughey lived in a James Gandon mansion on a 250 acre estate close to Dublin...and on a private island off the west coast..and in his yacht..and.....

But such was the legal climate at the time it was barely mentioned in the press. The day he actually retired in 1992, I was asked to do a special cartoon for the paper. It is reproduced below. It was never published. It was, according to the Irish Times lawyers, libelous. "But," I said, "it is true." "It may well be," they said,

"but can you afford the court case to prove it?"
And it wasn't just Haughey who could hide behind legalities to prevent the press from exposing the corruption endemic in the Republic's politics at the time. Magill magazine, I recall, was forever being injuncted on the eve of publication, to prevent publication of some story or other about some politician or other.

Haughey was like Marmite. People either loved him or hated him. When he resigned we brought out a limited edition book of Haughey cartoons. It was one of the worst publishing decisions ever made. We sold the 1,000 numbered copies in a day. It could have been the best seller I never had, nor will I ever have I hear you cry. I sold 400 copies in one afternoon at my first ever book signing at Fred Hanna's bookstore in Nassau Street. Nobody bought a copy for themselves. It was either "I am buying this for my wife/husband/brother/sister..she/he/it loves Charlie Haughey" or "I am buying this for my wife/husband/brother/sister. He/she/it hates Charlie Haughey". Emboldened by the public's apparent love of my works I repeated the exercise a few years later with a book about Albert Reynolds. I sold 35 copies in the whole afternoon. Back to the drawing board.

Haughey enjoyed living beyond his means, he enjoyed the arts and he enjoyed, apparently, the company of women. A friend of mine had persuaded Charles J to open an exhibition of watercolours at a gallery in Dublin. When he had done the honours, worked the room and left, my chum's wife was talking to some of her girlfriends. "And," she said "Charlie spoke to me. He talked about some of the pictures and then said, sotto voce, - 'I have to tell you that you are the best looking lady in the room'," "He said that to me too," said one of her friends.
 "And me."
"And me!"

The new 'portrait' I have done of Charlie is inspired, if that is the word, by a story told to me by a Dublin artist of some note. He recounted how he had once received the call that CJH wished to see him at Kinsealy. He wondered why. He turned up and was shown into an anteroom outside the study. The walls were covered in portraits and photographs of the great leader. There were sculptures and paintings but, as far as he could see, he told me, no cartoons. He was eventually ushered in to the study which was similarly decorated. CJ came swiftly to the point. "I would like," said the Taoiseach, surrounded by a cornucopia of his own images, "for you to paint my portrait."

He wasn't hard to draw. Big red nose, hooded eyes and a nice piece of hair that sprouted upwards, a lot more in my cartoons than in real life. I also gave him a nice solid pair of evil dark eyebrows which he didn't have in real life but looked somehow right in a cartoon. A perceptive reader once wrote to The Irish

Times to point out that my drawing of Ian Paisley was just a copy of my drawing of CJH but with different hair and jowls. He wasn't far wrong save that I was drawing Paisley long before Haughey came into view.

My favourite caricature of Charles Haughey was done by Andy Davey, the best underemployed caricaturist in Britain. The original of this drawing used to hang in the upstairs corridor of our house, just outside a spare bedroom. It was next to a gruesome, but delightful, Dave Brown cartoon of Sarkozy bursting out of Jacques Chirac's chest, in the style of that famous scene from Alien.

The family were staying and my son insisted that I took the Haughey caricature down and put it elsewhere. It was, apparently, giving the grandchildren nightmares.

They wouldn't walk past it to go to bed. They didn't mind the bloody Sarkozy image, just the drawing of Haughey.

In the 1960s Haughey successfully, sort of, sued the Sunday Independent over a cartoon by Warner (later to be famous in this parish as the creator of the O'Dearest cartoons which ran on the front page of the Irish Times for a while). The cartoon suggested that Haughey might have bribed a policeman to keep him away from a D&D charge. Of course, it was nonsense. Charlie never handed over a bribe, it was always the other way round.

But he was a grand lad for holding a grudge and trying to throw his weight around. The Irish Times rang me one day to tell me that they had been trying to get an interview with Haughey. He said he would be happy to do the interview on two conditions. One was that The Irish Times would sack Dick Walsh, the legendary political guru of the paper. And the second was that they would also sack the cartoonist. I was honoured to be in such exalted company. Felt great for weeks after that.

It was nice to know that he noticed. But no one ever accused Haughey of being stupid, or unaware, or unimaginative. In fact he had so many qualities, good and bad, he was truly larger than life, even if he was as small as Napoleon. He was thoughtful enough to mention me again in dispatches at a later date. Someone I had done some work for called one day to say he had just been walking along the seafront in Kinsale when he met Charlie. Charlie invited him on board his boat . They were having a drink and CJ asked "Well, what have you been up to lately?" "Not much," came the reply, "although I am about to open a new restaurant." "Oh," said Charlie, "anything different about it?" "Not really, oh, except I got Martyn Turner to do a load of drawings for the menu and wine list." There was a very sharp intake of breath and a slight glower from the former Taoiseach. The restaurateur realised that this might not have been the best thing to say to the politician, so he tried to backtrack a little. "Not that I know Martyn Turner," he said and then thought that he was being a tad disloyal to me so he added, in my support, "although he sounds very nice on the phone." "They say Hitler sounded nice on the phone," said Charlie.

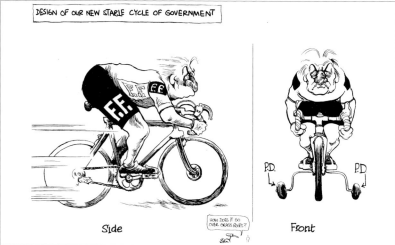

A Canadian cartoonist friend told me once that they had some sort of competition between the cartoonists to see how long they could go between using the titanic imagery in a cartoon. Sightings of the first Titanic cartoon of the year were treated with the reverence as that of the first sound of a cuckoo on the letters page.

It is hard to know how often you can use the same idea without it being obvious. My current rule of thumb, if I have an idea for a cartoon that seems familiar, is to go back one year and see if I drew it in that timespace. If not, I proceed.

Repetition, though, is often the lifeblood of comedy. Where would, say, The Fast Show have been without every week being identical to the week before. Most sitcoms rely on repetitive catch phrases, and so on.

Here are a couple of lookalike Charlie Haughey cartoons. I liked using them as they allude to my "I recognise you at once, you're the guy who won the tour de france" cartoon, one of my few jokes that worked.

p.s. for those of you who weren't there "Traynor" wheels refers to Des Traynor who was sometimes referred to as CJH's bagman inasmuch as he went round trawling funds for the great leader.

25

Garret FitzGerald

Garret FitzGerald was Taoiseach twice. The first was for just over 8 months from the end of June 1981 until the beginning of March 1982. He was then leader of another Fine Gael/Labour coalition from December 1982 until March 1987. Among his cabinet members were Alan Dukes (Fine Gael) and Dick Spring and Barry Desmond (Labour).

*O*f all the Taoisigh who have reigned under my watch, Garret FitzGerald is the only one I knew personally. Well, when I say "knew personally" what I mean is that I once had dinner at the same table as him at an awards ceremony (Fortnight magazine won the Ewart-Bigg Memorial Prize for fostering Anglo-Irish understanding not many people know that or, indeed, care) and I once bought him lunch in Galway. Well, when I say "bought him lunch" what I mean is that the restaurant where I was hanging an exhibition bought both of us lunch. Did either of us ever declare this largess to the appropriate authorities? Did we f*ck. Corruption knows no bounds. He was also one of *Fortnight's* Dublin correspondents in the early 1970s when I was *Fortnight's* co-editor. I can't remember talking to him on the phone begging for copy but I can remember being mortified when we/me (?) once described him as a member of 'Fianna Gael' in an article heading and it slipped through all our proofreading procedures. The ignorance of northerners about the south (and vice versa) knows no bounds.

I liked Garret FitzGerald. What wasn't there to not like? He wasn't called Garret the Good for nothing. This raises the question of how do you draw political cartoons criticising someone who you think is a decent bloke trying to do the right things? Many years ago I was at a cartoonist's shindig (note to the media at large - cartoonists do not have 'field days'. We have never had a field day and never plan to. We have shindigs, piss ups and, occasionally, festivals but never field days. Have we got that sorted? Good) in Budapest sitting on a panel with Paul Szep, then of the Boston Globe. A Hungarian cartoonist asked a question "We have just had our first democratic elections. How can I draw cartoons criticising someone who I have just voted for?" Paul said: "Don't worry. You'll learn. And very quickly".

Thus it was with Garret. Although I didn't vote for him. I have never been able to bring myself to give even a preference to either Fine Gael or Fianna Fáil when voting. But I welcomed his Constitutional Crusade. Not before time. The Constitution was, and is, a document of its time, written by deeply conservative and religious gents. Well past its sell by date.

And, while we are at it, I would baulk at the term "Crusade" as the Crusades were a quite disgusting 11th Century Church attempt to slaughter people in the name of some improbably existent deity. Whilst I would happily take the sword to many of the provisions of the Constitution, I will always be a bit squeamish about taking the sword to anything, human or animal, for any reason whatsoever. Call me, er, pro-life.

But to get back to the point. When you draw a Taoiseach or any other politician in a cartoon, it is never personal. It can't be an attack on the person as in 99.9 per cent of cases you don't know the person. All you know are his public utterances, his policies and his demeanour. And as Taoiseach that politician is responsible for everything his (or her - when, oh when, are we going to have a 'her'?) government does. Thus I draw Enda Kenny to represent government policy, or what I perceive as government policy, and the Government, not Enda Kenny as himself. He is just a symbol of everything his Government does, or doesn't do.

Thus it was with Garret. I wanted reform and I wanted it yesterday. I wanted changes in social welfare, tax codes and economic strategies and, being just a cartoonist, I had the luxury of not having to worry about the dire situation of the public finances when I demanded them. Bit like being in Opposition, really. Completely like being in Opposition actually. A complete and utter luxury. (Just wait to see what happens to Sinn Féin's economic policies when Baron Adams of Dundalk takes over at the helm of the ship of state.)

Thus one of my brief and rare moments of smug self satisfaction came when someone from RTÉ, John Bowman I think, rang up and suggested I listened to an interview they had recorded with Garret after he had left office. He told me that Garret had said that one of the hardest bits of government was to walk into a cabinet meeting with that day's *Irish Times* cartoon under his arm. I listened to the interview and never heard him say that. I guess it is on a cutting room floor somewhere. But I remember, oh yes indeed. I remember little else.

I recounted my one and only story about Garret - which he told me at our free lunch in Galway - in the paper three years ago. So those of you who remember move on at this point. For the record here it is again.

Garret and Maurice Manning were sitting in a hostelry in Dublin trying to think up ways to make Garret more exciting, less the figures and numbers and academic man he came across as. (It is claimed that Garret once actually said "I know that it works in practice but how will it work in theory?" It is probably apocryphal but none the worse for that.) They decided that they should invent a girlfriend for Garret and went about profiling this fictitious lady. Obviously, she should have not only an interest in statistics but be European, maybe something to do with airlines as Garret had an interest in such things. They were discussing this fair phantom when PJ Mara, Haughey's henchman, walked into the bar, spotted them and came over. "What are you two talking about?" asked PJ. "We were just discussing Garret's girlfriend," said Maurice Manning. "Ah, her," said Mara, "We've known about her for years."

TAKING A LEAF OUT OF THE DANISH BOOK — Our Politicians Act.

This drawing was done for The Saturday Column and I have included it here as it contains the images of three taoisigh, at various stages of their development.

From the left we have: Anon, Alan Dukes, Garret FitzGerald, Des O'Malley, Dick Spring, a Provo, Charlie Haughey, Alice Glenn (who was a strange mixture of right-wing Fine Gael, enthusiastic Roman Catholic and sort of street-wise Dubliner), Tomás Mac Giolla, John Bruton, Brian Lenihan Snr and Anon again.

The Saturday Column was edited for a while by Séamus Martin. At that time he and I used to write funny bits and oddities together to include in the column. Once, when Jack Charlton's, how can I call them, Anglo/Irish football team were doing well we devised a football team of Irish political heroes who were, like the real football team, born well outside the confines of the Republic of Ireland. It wasn't hard. Could have listed a rugby team. Everyone was born outside Ireland, including me, of course, although I am not a political hero (except in my own mind).

We managed, naturally, to get it wrong. We got a letter from a relative of one of our team pointing out that not only was his great great uncle born in Ireland (he fled when a babe in arms) but had become, subsequently, a man in arm as he lost one limb, poor devil, in an accident in a mill in Lancashire. I had drawn him with two arms. Luckily we hadn't put him in goal.

Séamus and I also did crystal ball predictions for the year ahead each January. Inspired by this, Trinity College library asked me to open an exhibition on Astrology. I said to them that Séamus would do it as I was physically incapable of opening my mouth in public unless seriously drugged. So we did it together. Seamus spoke and at the end, when he said "We declare this exhibition", I stepped forward and said, "Open".
That worked.

A lady came up to me afterwards and said she was very disappointed as she had come into Dublin to see me 'perform' and I hadn't drawn a thing and had only said one word.
But, I said, in my defence, I had, at least, written the speech that Séamus delivered.
"Of course you did, dear," she said, patting me gently on the forearm, "of course you did", and not believing a word of it.

The Taoiseach studying his lines en route to the EEC Summit

41

Albert Reynolds

Albert Reynolds was a TD for 25 years. He served as Taoiseach for two different governments. He took over from Charles Haughey as leader of Fianna Fáil in February 1992 and became, thus, Taoiseach in the Fianna Fáil/Progressive Democrat government. Following an inconclusive general election in the same year (November 25th), that Government ran until January 1993 after which he headed a Fianna Fáil/Labour administration until that fell apart in December 1994.

Albert Reynolds spent a shortish time running the country. But what it lacked as a result of brevity, it made up for in excitement. These were days when the distribution of seats between the various parties was such that all governments operated on wafer thin majorities.

The Progressive Democrats, formed from a rump of Fianna Fáilers who were disaffected with the overt armchair nationalism of Charles Haughey amongst other things, and who sought some sort of economic restructuring towards the 'free' market, were persuaded back, as it were, into the fold by coalescing with their erstwhile colleagues. They claimed that they were going to keep Fianna Fáil honest, a task Hercules himself would have baulked at. But, I guess, they tried.

Reynolds had much on his plate. Apart from a struggling economy he had to deal with the constitutional problems caused by the X case and also with the perennial sore that was Northern Ireland. And, of course, the split in his own party caused by the kerfuffle over the leadership. He brought to the task a lifetime of wheeling and dealing, firstly as a dance hall owner and latterly running numerous companies, the most notable of which canned dog food. In Haughey governments he had been the Minister for Industry and Commerce and, latterly, the Minister for Finance. He was Mr Business in a cowboy hat.

Reynolds was a joy for satirists and cartoonists. He spoke injudiciously describing coalition as a "temporary little arrangement". "That's women for you" was another of his catch phrases. Ah, those were the days (that's one of my own catch phrases, I think I stole it).

He was also hard work for satirists and cartoonists. Things moved so quickly at times, between intrigue and spats and rows and walk outs (and that is just the politicians) that what was drawn after breakfast could be torn up at lunchtime and what was drawn after lunch could be out of date by teatime.

At least, in those days, I could deliver drawings by fax machine and wasn't dependent upon the 6-o-clock bus from Kilcullen. The fax machine was the reason my drawings changed in shape from pretty well any shape or size to one that was a wide sausage shaped landscape. Fax machines only operated at 200 dpi and you really needed a bit more detail than that to produce a decent, or indecent for that matter, printable image.

Some fax machines operated on large rolls of paper rather than single A4 sheets. By producing a drawing that came out in D'Olier Street as a long roll it could be reduced down to some sort of printable quality and size.

I drew in that shape for years. Quite enjoyed it as you really had to think about the design of each drawing. It was a very good shape for my 500 word essayettes that crop up from time to time. If only I could be a cartoonist that just drew pictures.

But the intrigues of Albert, his relationships with his coalition partners, his deals and plans, got everyone talking about politics. It was better than television. I had a letter from someone saying her office used to meet for coffee at 11, open The Irish Times and discuss the cartoon and the situation.

Ah those were the days. Is there an echo in here?

John Bruton

John Bruton of Fine Gael took over from Albert Reynolds in December 1994. He formed a coalition with the Labour Party (which had resigned from Reynolds's cabinet) and Democratic Left (which later merged with the Labour Party). Their rainbow coalition lasted until late June 1997. His cabinet contained many Labour stalwarts: Dick Spring, Ruairi Quinn (Minister for Finance) and Michael D. Higgins (whatever happened to him?) as Minister for the Arts.

*J*ohn Bruton was/is something of an enigma. Seemingly old school Fine Gael, he nonetheless held a referendum to legalise divorce and, furthermore, eventually happily worked with not only the Labour Party but, quell horror, Democratic Left. Now, from the sidelines, he happily puts in his four pennyworth (well, it is usually someone else's fourpennyworth as he has amassed pensions of 140 grand a year and supplements his farming income with nixers from the world of finance and business) to tell us we should retrench and austeer (I invented this word, this very second) a path of fiscal rectitude for decades to come.

He is devotedly European, even the Social Democrat Europe, not just the Angela Merkel Europe and he looked beyond the narrowness of Irish politics to embrace, non-fortuitously as it turned out, the British Royal family and them Brits in general. Good for him.

He fell out of coalition with the Labour Party twice. Once when as Minister for Finance he produced a budget that caused Jim Kemmy (then an independent, later a member of the Labour Party) to withdraw his support and consequently the Labour/Fine Gael government collapsed. And once, after an inconclusive General Election late in 1992 when he failed to reach agreement with Labour who promptly fell in with Fianna Fáil.

When Labour then later fell out with Fianna Fáil, Bruton fell into government. Not only with Labour but with Democratic Left, a party he had vowed never to go into government with, with whom he had vowed to never go into government for the pedants out there.

If you are to believe the pundits, there is general agreement that his left/right government was ok, pretty good, not bad, could have been worse. The voting public were so impressed that the next three governments were all Fianna Fáil led. But that is voters for you. No sooner are we told, for example, that Ruairi Quinn is the best Minister for Finance the State ever had than he has to cling on to his parliamentary seat by his fingertips for the next two decades and, when he does eventually get back into government, is forced into resignation just when he had started to get to grips with a recalcitrant Church and an equally recalcitrant teaching profession. That's politics for you.

In the rather insular world of Irish political cartooning, I had to come to grips with drawing the sort of grey and soft Mr Bruton. Unlike my chums who work in Britain, or the States, or pretty well anywhere else, there aren't enough of us plying our trade to arrive at a consensus of how politicians should be drawn. In other words we can't steal from each other. I had no problem with the Labourites as they had been around for a while and Dick Spring was kind enough to grow a moustache and Ruairi Quinn, like Michael Noonan nowadays, has a boiled egg for a head. Even I can draw boiled eggs.

Bruton's predecessor Alan Dukes was also an easy draw. Excessively tall (almost as tall as me - is this possible?) he could be excluded from some drawings as he was up in the clouds. Of course the clouds were of his own making as he smoked all the time, the beast. I HATE smoking. I took to putting cigarettes in the ears of politicians who smoke. No, I don't know why either, but I just did. Alright? I think Dukes was the first. Maybe Des O'Malley. Cowen and Obama followed. He told me once as he stared up into my face, hovering, as it did, half an inch over his, that he was once tempted to walk out on a platform with a cigarette stuck in his ear, a la cartoon, so people would recognise him.

But John Bruton had none of these 'assets'. His most noticeable feature was a braying laugh that would cause hyenas to flee, elephants to stampede and small children to hide under sofas. But, fair dues, he laughed. Give me a politician who laughs (Bruton, Paisley, et Al - that's Albert) any day over politicians who deadpan through life (Cosgrave, Enoch Powell - yes I'm that old - or Gerry Adams). So I drew him with an inane smile all the time. That seemed to work. And then I added, having seen Steve Bell's drawing of Norman Tebbit in the Guardian, a motorcycle helmet forehead with two emerging eyes underneath. It wasn't great but it was mine.

Bertie Ahern

Bertie Ahern (Patrick Bartholomew, apparently) was Taoiseach from the end of June 1997 until May 2008. He took over the leadership of Fianna Fáil from Albert Reynolds in November 1994. He was minister for finance from November 1991 until December 1994.

$\mathcal{B}$ertie Ahern. You couldn't make him up. Although, truth be told, I think he did. Make himself up. I have a feeling he claimed to be an accountant, to have gone to university (UCD? LSE?) although I've never seen any record of either. He did go to the College of Commerce in Rathmines and he did work as a book keeper at the Mater hospital. So he knew about numbers. And he knew enough about banks to not have a bank account when he was minister for finance. He had a safe, in Drumcondra. Details of his attitude to both his own finances and others emerged in dribs and drabs during both the Moriarty Tribunal and the Mahon Tribunal. He famously signed blank cheques for Charlie Haughey when Ahern was Fianna Fáil's treasurer.

The stories from the planning tribunal about the culture within Fianna Fáil read like a badly plotted satirical novel. No one would have believed half of what went on. It is quite difficult to be a satirist when Fianna Fáil is in office. No sooner have you made up some improbable scenario than it turns out to be true. I once experienced Fianna Fáil culture first hand. Bizarrely I was rung by FF HQ and asked if I could do a drawing for them. I said "Are you sure you have the right number?" But they said they did. Someone was leaving or had a political anniversary or somesuch and they wanted to present him with a cartoon, drawn by me, of him. Go figure. Anyway I agreed to do the drawing and they agreed to pay me. I did the drawing. They arrived at my house to collect it. I handed over the drawing. And an invoice. The invoice was declined. "Here", they said, handing over a brown envelope full of cash. A real brown envelope. I should have had it framed. Just like at the Tribunals. When they had gone I counted it for some reason. I usually just hand over what Joyce Grenfell used to call "the sordid coin" to management straight away. But this time I counted it. It was short a few quid.

Bertie was an enthusiast for "light touch regulation". Light touch, it turned out, came from that phrase "light touch paper and retire". Which he did. After the economy had been wrecked by light touch, or no touch, regulation.

Mr Ahern had the gift of the gobbledegook. He seems to have tried to kiss the Blarney stone but missed and got some other stone that offered malapropisms, obfuscation and vagueness. It was quite a joy to listen to. I guess "smoke and daggers" was the most famous catchphrase. You sort of knew what he meant if you didn't think about it too carefully.

He also claimed to be a socialist. I remember that one. He said it in the Dáil. Surprisingly, then, he forsook the chance to bring Labour (sort of socialist) into government after the 2007 general election, choosing instead to hook up once again with the Progressive Democrats (the anathema of socialism).

Charlie Haughey once claimed Bertie was the most Machiavellian of them all. He later said the expression was taken out of context, misunderstood. Of course the term "Machiavellian" is always taken out of context. Machiavelli was quite a decent sort; philosopher, diplomat, ethicist. The "Machiavellian" bit of Machiavelli was in the title character in his work "The Prince". So maybe Bertie was a Crown Prince, or Clown Prince anyway.

I must say I enjoyed the Bertie years. He had a great uniform, yellow suits and anoraks and, thanks to the tribunals, he was a politician who just went on giving. Like Albert before him he had an instinctive eye for the deal. It served him well when dealing with Tony Blair and them Northern Ireland types. Despite being chucked out of Fianna Fáil he still has some sort of reputation abroad and makes speeches and attempts peace deals in foreign parts from time to time.

I don't know whether he has got round to getting a bank account yet.

1997

This cartoon of Ray Burke, later convicted for tax fraud, but implicated in various charges of getting hand outs, was held out of the paper by The Irish Times lawyers as late as 1997 because the double entendre of Burke, a politician cum auctioneer or vice versa, standing by a sign reading "For Sale" was too much to stomach, legally. Our chronically one sided libel laws can take part of the blame for the slow uncovering of political corruption in the State.

Similarly by introducing blasphemy laws as recently as 2009 we seem to be somewhat out of step, free speech wise, with the rest of Europe. Jesus Wept..can I say that?

1998

PERCEPTION of the GOVERNMENT **BEFORE** THOUSANDS of PUNTS SPENT on P.R., IMAGE CONSULTANTS, BEAUTICIANS etc...

PERCEPTION of the GOVERNMENT **AFTER** THOUSANDS of PUNTS SPENT on P.R., IMAGE CONSULTANTS, BEAUTICIANS etc...

IT'S SHOCKING TO SEE THE GARDAI HAVING TO RESORT TO SUBTERFUGE, UNTRUTHS AND "INDUSTRIAL ACTION" TO GET THEIR PAY CLAIM.....

...WE DID NOTHING TO GET OURS.....

T.D. & MINISTERIAL PAY RISES & BACK PAY

INCREASED T.D. EXPENSES

AND YOU'LL PROBABLY GO ON DOING NOTHING..

1999

2000

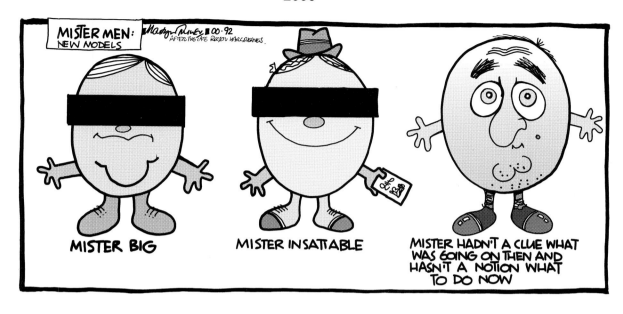

2001

2001

2002

2003

2003

2011

2012

2014

Brian Cowen

Brian Cowen was Taoiseach from May 2008 until March 2011, head of a coalition between his own party, Fianna Fáil, and the Green Party and the Progressive Democrats/Independents. He was a TD for 27 years.

*B*rian Cowen's Reign of Error (sounds like a rock band) is fresh enough in the memory of us all for it to need little comment or elucidation from me. Not that this is going to stop me as I have a book to fill, and a contractual obligation to fill it with daft words as well as daft pictures.

Brian Cowen differed from his immediate predecessors as Fianna Fáil leader inasmuch as he didn't have the whiff of cordite or the aroma of the deals of the gombeen, or the stain of brown envelopes attached to his character. He was just a boorish country solicitor who had risen through the ranks of the party and, on the way, filled pretty well every cabinet post on offer. Towards the end of his parliamentary existence I think he filled half a dozen cabinet posts on his own while all his erstwhile chums fled the sinking ship.

As minister for health he famously referred to his brief as 'Angola' .By which he meant that it was formerly colonised by the Portuguese? That it had a whole bunch of official languages and ethnic and tribal divisions? That it was riven with civil war? Close. Apparently it was because you didn't know where the next explosion was coming from. Angola is full of unexploded mines, it seems. Like half the world. Well, arms manufacturers have to make a living too, unfortunately, although personally I would question this assumption.

So watch where you tread next time you visit the HSE. Remember what Brian said.

He took over from Bertie Ahern as chief of Fianna Fáil by party acclamation. It was his destiny. An eerie parallel between his coronation and career and that of Gordon Brown, of the British Labour party, exists. Both were destined for the top job and were welcomed when they finally got it only to blow up, quickly, in a explosive cloud of failure and public opprobrium. Like stepping on a mine, figuratively, like in, er, Angola.

Also like Gordon Brown, he probably wasn't responsible for his own perceived failure. He was the wrong man at the wrong time. It is hard to imagine that there was a right man although I'm sure many, even people who aren't political cartoonists, could have told him how to make a better fist of things. He could have nationalised the banks a bit earlier. He could have let Anglo-Irish go down the Swanee and let the bondholders go into penury instead of letting the country go into penury. He could, maybe, have seen things coming and not presided over the greatest giveaway budgets in the history of the State when he was Minister for Finance. He could have had a political policy, a basic plan, instead of flying by the seat of his outsized pants. But then he would have had to be in a different political party. Fianna Fáil didn't get where it is today by having an ethos other than "Up ya boya". Just being nice enough, nationalist enough, scary enough to win the next election always did for them. A chameleon of politics blending in perfectly with whatever they thought the public mood was. Works fine until something goes wrong.

For the cartoonist, Brian Cowen was a gift. Anyone who can be slagged off by Ian Paisley for his appearance had to be a gift. Talk about pots and kettles. His features were Paisleyesque inasmuch as they were larger than life. His manner, described as brusque, rude, and off hand didn't help. His love of the family business, politics and pubs, added to the character. He sang in public. Never a great idea for the politician. Those of us of ancient vintage remember Peter Brooke singing "My Darling Clementine" on the Late Late Show and doing for his political career in the process. Brian Cowen sang "The Lakes of Ponchartrain" at 3 in the morning after a few gargles and then managed an interview on breakfast radio a few hours later. That didn't work out well, either.

I never met Brian Cowen but our eyes did meet across a crowded bar once at Navan racecourse. He glowered, I think, having just been told who that vast overgrown idiot on the other side of the room was by Jim McDaid, then a TD, with whom I had been talking. I hope it was a glower. It may have been a look of boredom or annoyance (their horse had just lost). He may have just been staring past me out of the window at the parade ring. I'm sure it was a glower. I deserved a glower at least.

Like Gordon Brown, Brian Cowen was something of a disappointment. He suffered awfully from bad timing and from situations that he brought on himself in large part. But he came across as morose and grumpy and downright uncommunicative whereas, we were told, in private, he was a fabled joke teller and mimic with caustic wit. We saw precious little of that. Pity. We could have done with a laugh in those days.

2008

2009

2009

2009

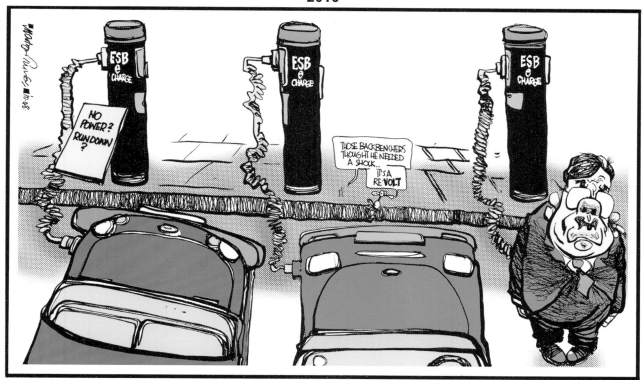

2010

2010

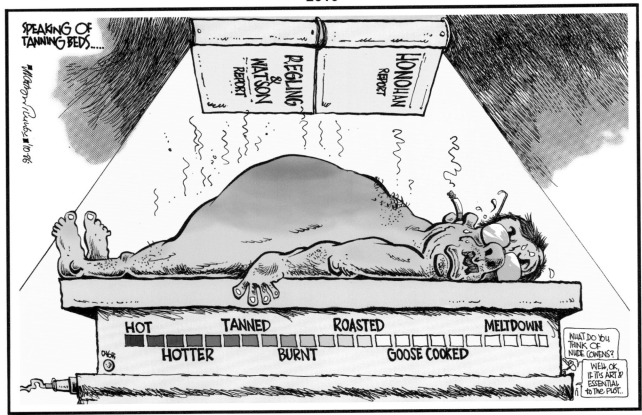

Enda Kenny

Enda Kenny has been Taoiseach since March 2011, in coalition with the Labour Party. He was the longest serving TD in the Dáil at the time of his appointment (which means, ergo, he still is).

nda Kenny has been Taoiseach since March 2011, in coalition with the Labour Party. He was the longest serving TD in the Dáil at the time of his appointment (which means, ergo, he still is).

Enda is still in charge as I write this, in August 2014. It isn't raining but the promised heatwave hasn't arrived. Oh, sorry, where was I? Enda. Oh yes, still in charge but there is a tricky Budget coming up, what with the new Labour leader an' all, so if he is gone by the time this is published feel free to add, in black pen only, to the notation above. Of course you can't return books that have been defaced. So, please, go ahead.

Enda is, if nothing else, a survivor. He took over as leader of Fine Gael from Michael Noonan in June 2002 and survived a few attempted heaves from bands of dissidents meeting in a hotel somewhere off the Naas Road. The usual. He survived, thus, he is a survivor. It's easy this political commentary, isn't it. His Taoiseachacy (the words I have to make up, endless) was made all the easier as his government adopted the Fianna Fáil economic plan, lock, stock and two smoking barrels.

But he married into Fianna Fáil so I guess it was easy enough to adopt their policies, which, of course, weren't their policies but those dictated to them by a very nice Indian man from the IMF who walked happily around Dublin for a while and then overcharged us for the bailout.

Aside from bailing out banks and charging us for the pleasure of doing it, he has tackled the ongoing sore of the Catholic Church, and the way they might abuse you, by being a regular human being and standing up to them, a bit, sort of. Quite impressive there for a moment. Of course while harsh words were spoken, very little has been done and we, when not bailing out the banks, bail out the Church as it begrudgingly makes reparations to the thousands it has destroyed with its activities. But ignore me, I'm just a heathen bigot, it says in the Letters page of The Irish Times, so it must be true.

Cartoon-wise, he is/was a slippery customer. Doesn't really look like anything caricaturable. Something of a let-down after the joys of Albert, Bertie and Biffo. Now there were politicians who knew how to help cartoonists and caricaturists. Piece of piss (this is not a reference to their characters, just a term which means "quite easy". Australian slang term, apparently, if you want to know its derivation, cobber) they were. A joy.

Enda isn't. He looks younger than his years. He runs. He cycles. He looks after himself. This is quite out of character with previous incumbents of the office. He'll probably last forever, or be slung out on his ear at the next election in favour of some guy who I can't draw who was in the last Fianna Fáil cabinet and Baron Adams of the Duchy of Dundalk. That'll be the next book, then.

2011

2012

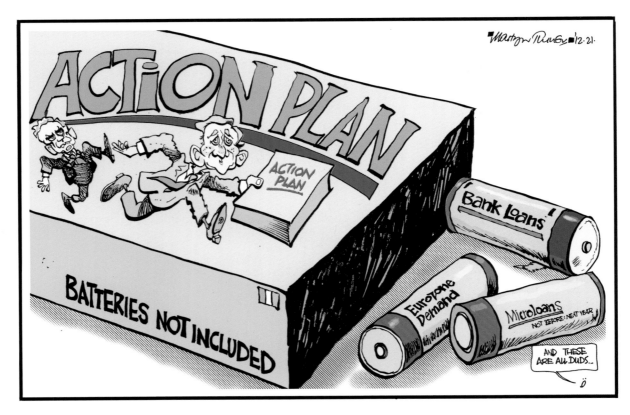

2012

2012

131

2012

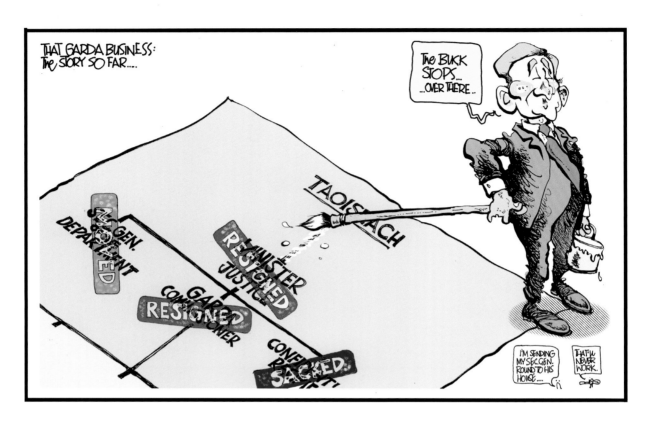

This is the cartoon that Enda never appeared in. After the disastrous election results of May 2014 I was trying to draw a cartoon suggesting that the two coalition leaders were lame ducks. after I had sent the cartoon off, the leader of the Labour Party, Eamon Gilmore, took it upon himself to resign, before he was pushed. I was on my second glass of wine at that stage so rather than think afresh I amended. Actually, of course, it was more apposite as the "Way" phrase was Eamon's not Enda's.